Table of Contents

Rourke
Educational Media
rourkeeducationalmedia.com

Can you find these words?

beet

crepes

pretzels

seaweed

What We Eat

Where do you live? What do you eat?

In Central America, people eat rice with black beans.

People eat **crepes** in France.

crepes

People eat **beet** soup in Poland.

beet

It is served cold.

People in Germany eat **pretzels.**

pretzels

People in Japan eat fish and rice.

They also eat **seaweed.** It is healthy!

seaweed

Did you find these words?

People eat **beet** soup in Poland.

People eat **crepes** in France.

People in Germany eat **pretzels**.

They also eat **seaweed**.

Photo Glossary

 **beet** (beet): A dark red root vegetable.

 **crepes** (kraypes): Very thin pancakes that often have a filling.

 **pretzels** (PRET-suhlz): Dough shaped into knots and baked until crispy.

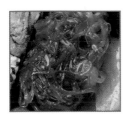 **seaweed** (SEE-weed): Plants that grow in the oceans, rivers, and other bodies of water.

Index

About the Author

Katy Duffield is a writer who likes to eat. She's never tried beet soup or seaweed. But she loves crepes and rice and beans. Her very favorite food is PIZZA!

www.rourkeeducationalmedia.com

PHOTO CREDITS: Cover ©hanapon1002, Page 3 ©By Africa Studio, Page 4 ©MSPhotographic, Page 5 ©Yul, Page 6 ©Yul , Page 9 ©Stevenchock, Page 10 ©Yul, Page 12 © Yul, Page 2,10-11,14,15 ©dallosto, Page 2,12-13,14,15 ©Milkos, Page 2,6-7,14,15 ©Yulia_Davidovich, Page 2,8-9,14,15 ©LarisaBlinova

Edited by: Keli Sipperley
Cover design by: Kathy Walsh
Interior design by: Rhea Magaro-Wallace

Library of Congress PCN Data
What We Eat / Katy Duffield
(Let's Find Out)
ISBN (hard cover)(alk. paper) 978-1-64156-191-4
ISBN (soft cover) 978-1-64156-247-8
ISBN (e-Book) 978-1-64156-297-3
Library of Congress Control Number: 2017957801

Printed in the United States of America, North Mankato, Minnesota